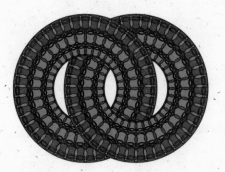

ABLOOM

&

AWRY

ABLOOM

&

AWRY

TINA

KELLEY

CavanKerry ❖ Press LTD.

CavanKerry Press Ltd.
Fort Lee, New Jersey
www.cavankerrypress.org

Publisher's Cataloging-in-Publication
(Provided by Quality Books, Inc.)

    Kelley, Tina, author.
      [Poems. Selections]
      Abloom & awry / Tina Kelley.
      pages cm
      ISBN 978-1-933880-61-7
      1. Families—Poetry. 2. Motherhood—Poetry.
      3. Poetry.   I. Title. II. Title: Abloom and awry.
      PS3611.E443253A6 2017   811'.6
          QBI17-132

Cover artwork: "Flare Blare" by Gray Jacobik
Cover and interior text design by Ryan Scheife, Mayfly Design
First Edition 2017, Printed in the United States of America

CavanKerry Press is proud to present the first book in the Florenz Eisman Memorial Series—fine collections by New Jersey poets, notable or emerging. A gifted poet and great lover of poetry herself, Florenz was the publisher's partner in establishing CavanKerry and its Managing Editor from the press's inception in 2000 until her passing in 2013. Florenz's ideas and intelligence were a great source of inspiration for writers and staff alike as were her quick wit and signature red lipstick.

CavanKerry Press is grateful for the support it receives from the New Jersey State Council on the Arts.

Also by Tina Kelley

Precise, 2013

Almost Home: Helping Kids Move from Homelessness to Hope, 2012
(co-author)

The Gospel of Galore, 2003

To Pete, who has made it possible

CONTENTS

3. Ghosts of Good News

4. Illegible Smiles

Finale

ABLOOM

&

AWRY

PRELUDE

The Possible Utility of Poets

"As we are affected and altered by the living earth, I believe the earth is altered by the words we choose to use as we experience its lives and its features."

—Pattiann Rogers, "Under the Open Sky—
Poems on the Land," *Terrain* magazine, Fall/Winter 2011.

How often do we notice a star in a night? It matters.
Know your family tree of trees, which ones sheltered, shaped you.
For if I use tone-deaf metaphors, the second or third easiest thought,

the ground shudders, cracks deepen. Asparagus farmers are natural acolytes,
weeding fronds luxuriant with dew. The earth blooms a full inch when my son
explains, "A noun is basically everything. We can't go anywhere without nouns.

They're always next to us," and when my daughter asks, "What does
the moon mean?" and when I contemplate aqua, my favorite crayon,
its lagoons and flower centers, and yes when you give an extra paragraph

of thought to your deep love of dark-chocolate-covered sea salt caramels.
To keep the earth fertile, we must hike through rain, must watch more closely,
even on muggy days. Smell the dry spice of home, the viny weeds

that grew in our town's grass but nowhere since. I propose new definitions
of prayer: Beachcombing. Birding. Biking to work. Extra credit for imagining
a snow caterpillar, or lightning a foot deep. The best disciples memorialize

small differences, rare views into words: Marcescence: the retention of dead
plant organs normally shed; see oak, see beech. Katabatic: of or relating to wind
produced by cold dense air flowing down a mountain slope or glacier.

Paint a room in gradations of twilight. Maybe Earth's an only child
demanding attention, for so long the one planet supporting life.
Small price for the smell of hair just in from a winter walk.

So I will craft an amulet, a silver exclamation mark,
her birthstone the amethyst dot, connected by adamant
reverence, for all of us to wear and to hold, always.

Yawp

Read this love letter to life. Its pages turn in the ice-fling
off of the fast car's roof. Follow the traveling carillon,
the communism of the gospels, the ice rink's joyful
four-fold spotlight, how it shines the hair and adds grace.

Eyes and words swerve into focus, nouns marry in metaphor,
lines enter a stranger's memory and stay for seven years.

Smell the multiflora roses, honeysuckle, burning leaves.
Feel the inside of the body, the smooth core, watch the wren
pull the dead fledgling from the hole feather by dusty feather.
Guess the stories: tailless squirrel on the woodpile, condom

under the old folks home sofa, the lady's internal monologue
as she guards the Lamborghini at the auto show, red guts spilt

like berries from rabbit mouth. I'd write even if each page's
only destination were the stove, for winter heat. Again and again.

On Leaving the Newsroom

It is magic, writing news. We have an honored front row seat in life,
the chance to walk through the bat cave for six hours seeing the last
ceilingsful of brown bats mysteriously dying. What a privilege to listen
to someone tell of brain injury, grief, monster trucks or false imprisonment.
A gift to read the actual suicide note, hear about a beau who's "the cowboy kind
of quiet," watch the drips fall off Michael Phelps' perfect shoulders, hear "good luck"
from the flood victims who need it more than we do, attend a Nocturnal Bird Migration
Concert, know a little bit about just about everything, start with rumors and end with reality,
swear by precision, become incapable of fibbing, ask with abandon, and take notes
on talkers more profound than any of our imaginations, then
distill, discuss, dither over it and hit Send,
so a million can know what we learned.

Here I heard Mohamed Atta's eyes looked so dark,
no one could see his pupils. Here I learned of the girl
who would not take off her father's necktie, because
it smelled like him, before he rushed into the burning tower.

You can't buy a front row seat like that, a priceless seat, rarer
and rarer. And for twenty years they paid me to sit, or stand,
or run, or sprint, and use that keyboard. So few are this lucky.

HERE'S AN ARMFUL

My Man, the Green Man

*Pyrotechnicians known as Green Men would wear costumes of leaves and mud to
protect them from stray sparks and remain hidden from the crowds at firework displays.*

He covers himself in clay and branches,
hidden in what protects him best:
dusky blanket, shadow, damp armor
against spiteful sparks or just one
watcher's *hmph* of disenchantment.

The crowd will never see my fine
firework-starter as he runs from fuse
to fuse, lighting sulfurous snakes,
thrusting delight to the skies,
higher than any have climbed

(though he takes me there, he does).
When he and his mates part, they say,
"Stay green"—safe, invisible, fertile,
invincible, wreathed in rainforest mist,
one redolent color and scent. I fell

when I caught the campfire light in his,
yes, green eyes, light his leaves give back,
those leaves leaking magic, the leaves
beekeepers-who-have-touched-the-dead
wash with before returning to the hive.

See how he calms my bag-of-cats temper,
soothes my brittle humors, douses anger
with wit, so laughter melts me in a sodden
clump. He can charm cranky children,
extinguish frustrations, smother spats.

He causes all that sparking glory, yet
stays blended in, self-effacing, green
saint of smoke. Coming home to the dark
still room, he smells of spent coals.
I hug the leafy cloak, and he pulls me in.

When I rest my hair in his moss,
I revel, remembering that rainstorm
when we could not have gotten wetter.
He saves one last pinwheel rocket
for me. We drench each other.

I worry, yes. He could vanish
in a flash. But he comes from a tall
line of tree-herders, patient, wet
behind the ears, therefore humbly wise,
deserving every ooh and ahhhh.

Come, let's ignite joy, create it
from bow drill and tinderbox,
burn the combustibles, soak
stinging cinders in sap, quench
ourselves in constancy, in camouflage.

Love Song to Boredom

The placid ennui of toilet-bowl water.
Pachysandra, impatiens, the somnambulation of team-building meetings.
Only an infinite and immutable object—that is, God himself—can fill this infinite abyss,
said Pascal. *Much of the time I sit around doing nothing,* said the Boredom Proneness Scale.

Over two decades, people really bored at work are twice as likely to die of a heart attack.
Some physicists believe time will slow, eventually disappear, and leave
the universe frozen "like a snapshot of one instant, forever,"
rallentando'd down, an eternal car parts ad.

But before all that, boredom, lift me up. Inspire me.
"You have to get to the point of boredom and then get past that,"
the photographer explained. Get the safe pictures out of your system
for the first three or four days, "and that's where the creativity starts."

Beloved, you're the emails from the guy who marks everything urgent. Unending
weeks of Pentecost. Catalog clothes and expense reports. Seventh-graders sing-
songing the pledge, third-graders practicing recorders. Almost every last
black dress at every cocktail party. Tax season. License renewals.

Only after: opal glint in the tarnished bracelet, one phrase in that awful novel,
the second attempt at the recital, the caper among the canned black olives.
The quirk, vigor, sparks from beige. You took me
to the yawning edge, and pushed.

The Meadow Saffron Said My Best Days Fled

I sent a bouquet, hoping you would read the blooms
in the right order (the logic, the crescendo, crucial):

Ranunculus	I am dazzled by your charms.
Diosma	Your simple elegance enthralls me.
Daphne odora	I would not have you otherwise.
Stock	You'll always be beautiful to me.
White violet	Let's take a chance on happiness.
Spider flower	Elope with me.

Of course, these never bloom at the same season.

I believe you are a fern: magic, fascination, confidence, shelter,
all in one stem. But fern means *Maybe* as well. Do not answer
Fern. You sent a leaf rose, *You may hope.*

Why is bittersweet truth? Why is honesty forgetfulness?
Because memory is deceitful, and lies have lovely petals.

Which flower means to lie in bed all afternoon, past dusk,
coupling over and over like it was our first and last chance?
That would be the peony, obviously. Magenta.

Other flowers are equally adamant. If any bloom ever said
Take off your clothes now, it's the iris, stretching upwards
and outwards, yearning towards touch. Here's an armful.

There are too few verbs in this language of flowers.
I propose the coral begonia: Run daily errands with me,
and cream day lily: Leave a pretty corpse.

None denote silliness or giddiness, which I need for love
the way I need music to have a satisfying cry.
The Johnny-jump-up, for its sheer tiny verve, suffices.

Five years in, I will send you a bouquet of Love-in-a-mist,
for Scratch a little lower, sugar. Months later, a sprig
of butterfly bush hints Give me more children.

Let's say the daffodil is for excellence in fatherhood,
the gazania, long-lasting, its stem in a plastic sheath,
is to remind dear friends of the joys of staying single.

But no flower, none, can mean No or Never.
And none has the eloquence to say outright
I wish I had told you more often how I love you.

Music Is an Underground River That Needs to Be Discovered

—Philip Glass

The tune swallows its tail, a rich soundtrack for a movie of me sculling,
though I've never tried rowing, never wanted to. The anthem drove me
to work, started that overdue sobbing fit, formed the bass line to bliss, or
proclaimed that no one would keep me down for long. Not the monotonous

brainworm, ricketytick banjo, or ballad conjuring bus tourists. Yes the milk-smooth
chant of the glee club, stately harmonies, progressions soaring: the song of my breath
when it smells cleanest, my fingerprint in good work. I fell down the well and found it,
strong current. The notes swoop from yellow to green, fold in, flowing. I hear the tune

again the next day, mistake it for an oldie, just as I recognized you when we first met.
It jumpstarts my pulse, puts the swing in my hips, gets me through chores. Music seeps
over a scene and reaches spots I couldn't touch with bland, silent words. Listen to the sounds
produced by the body—I know the word for that, *auscultation*. Listen as closely to wind,

wood thrushes, first evening star's less-than-plink, seismic motion, bell towers.
And a new favorite song will say once again: yes, this is my life.

Covalent

Pairs don't survive me. Socks, especially hand-knit,
are single after four washings. He who needs *that*
particular shin pad crumples in hysteria just before
the carpool arrives. One walkie-talkie has nothing

to listen to. Ear plugs rent asunder, toy cars stalled,
stilled junk without remote controls, under my care.
The drawers on various floors become diasporas:
puzzle pieces, a salt shaker, a flip-flop. How I dread

Mom's silver, smug in velvet-lined completeness.
The eye of my storm spit out one marriage, a new
griddle missing its plug, 14 decks of 51 cards, plus
a camera without a charger. Lucky I never had twins.

But what if all this splaying results from, reacts to,
the sturdiness of our union, my one, my solid man?
With you, centripetal and centrifugal find balance,
all potential bonding in the house has become a string

between us, not between mittens. You call to suggest
the new plan I've hatched, we buy the same funny card
to commemorate proposing to each other, and I must
rest my foot on some part of you to fall asleep at all.

Abloom & Awry

God lurks in the story of stethoscope,
kaleidoscope, microscope, but also in the punched
ache of falling apart: accidents, insanities, plot twists
surpassing human imagination. God's the sparrow
in the convention center, the skateboard akimbo
on the freeway shoulder, the perfect paw
reaching out of the long-flat roadkill, and somehow
the father shooting his two daughters, third wife
and self, leaving the baby son safe asleep.
God is all those lost, up in the God world
being nothing, stuck between the notes.

I worship the grape molding in the bunch's depths,
our neighbors' ruttings and fights our baby monitor
picks up, the metastasis of laughter, cauterization
of grief, that maroon bog-shininess of ancient remains,
the magnificat of dew on lady's mantle leaf, the cousin
born with *fetus in fetu*, her twin parasitizing her ovary,
the first caveman to huck a rock at his chum's skull,
the walk Joe took, alone, to spread his arm's ashes,
the cruelty young boys show to turtles, the suicidality
of child molesters, even pustard, that liquid dripping
from the bottle when all you really want is mustard.

I worship weird domestic ways to die,
electrocution by love song falling in bathtub,
infant decapitation by ceiling fan, while I praise
ways to create, painting with menstrual blood
on cave walls, Zen sand art by kitty in litter,
painted toddler feet tromping on the ceiling.

I worship every reason I cried this year,
slow songs, missing Dad, children refusing
to come downstairs for their special pancakes,
adoptive mother heartbroken at a son's sins,
also every new song I loved this year, but
most of all, if I may see, the many years to come.

The Next Creation of the Universe

After it was all over, time
stretched ahead like the cold black road
in front of the forty-car pileup.

After an exceedingly long wait,
longer than all definitions of long,
I try again, during the egg month.

I have kept many fine tiny building blocks:
stars, wind, peanut butter and chocolate.
I hum the sound of the well-warming world,

the pulse of sap ascending.
I shout favorite things: fulfilled potential,
wild generous nurture, swift imagination!

Laughter. I make female first, she does the rest.
(Honestly, why hasn't *anyone*
figured that out yet?)

I keep the hummingbirds, but they finally
feel sated. They relax a bit, stop making us
so damned concerned about them.

I let your devoted pets live as long as you do.
I give clear guidelines about religion: one,
voluntary, aiming for love and the full growth

of each follower. And of each who chooses
not to follow. I leave out committees, tumors,
corporations, lobbyists, mosquitoes, pro football.

I put a bell tower in every town, plus professional
harmonica players, photographers, masseuses,
reporters, and comedians. Many academics,

no academia—no committees, remember?
The rivers around Manhattan run roaring, not flat,
to match the city. Each moth has its own song.

Just before you die I get to tell you, OK, this
is what you were supposed to be, a composer
with five foster kids, and you should have married

that guy in St. Paul, and let your folks move in.
Every kitchen implement works as completely
and elegantly as my thick, solid spatula.

Strawberries and dried peaches smell better.
I'd invent more verbs for the sun than shine,
stream, rise, set, hide, blaze, and glow.

I call musical chairs illegal, to save five-year-olds
that cruel moment of losing face on center stage.
Japanese maples, smoked almonds, and waltzes prevail,

and I sit back and watch, flipping channels,
country to country, drama to musical comedy.
How long can you let this universe last?

Letter Written with the Kruger Brothers Picking in the Background

Dear One, So Saturday we finally
could make the trip up 18 North
to see Sairah, fresh from surgery.

And I smelled a tinge of cigar smoke
as we drove up through bright trees
like heaven on fire, up along the
Yadkin River. I couldn't wait
to hear the four family fiddles,
the neighbor's banjo, the intricate
music they breathe out, smiling,
never exactly the same again.

I felt so at home in the world,
feet up on the truck's dash while
Pete drove, but what does it mean
to be at home in a world that pushes
my loved ones out? It's just
two months since Eli passed,
ten months since Sairah's diagnosis.

The late sun hit popcorn clouds,
dyeing them every deep color
found in a clamshell, the sky beyond
as pure as a one-facet jewel,
and I had the sense of something
just starting to turn, like food,
almost about to go bad, to end.

I knew Pete wanted to be fishing
that rich river, but he's had my back,
and besides he's fond of the aunts
and cousins and babies, especially
Maya born fine, after Mae's stillbirth.

We felt so glad to see Sairah,
pale but lively, and I was in awe.
Cancer, at her young age, turns you
on your back, under the guillotine,
looking up at the blade, while we
who know we'll die of something
someday, maybe sudden, can turn
our faces and minds away for years.

This is the definition of prayer,
this gathering in, ringing ourselves
and our well-wishes around her bed
in the living room, tapping to the songs
that sing yes to forever. And I thought
of the word Graham just taught me,
saeculum, the amount of time between
an event and the death of its last witness.

And when Maya's gone, so much
of this will have gone, the banjos, leaves,
the scent of cigar. The pickup, griefs,
guillotine rope, maybe the music.
But please, not the river,
not the music.

Theophany, or Staying Home from Church to Write

The weather today is holy,
the opposite of hurricane, a high
pressure system dancing in dry air,
and the trees look all ticklish with warblers.
The divine is the ding in my windshield,
present in all moving, all seeing.

Hallowed how honeybees drink flowers all day.
Sacred, whatever it is about seven
that makes the seventh wave bigger.

When I am making a casserole
for the girls who lost their father,
it is someone else's grief, and communion,
and the onions, that make me cry.

Ever blessed: the chocolate-smooth
feel of writing in pencil.

Can you catch leaves on the way down?
The kids tried, and I joined them. We failed,
but worship wheeled and reeled.

It lives in the daily intercessions the dog's nose
leaves in strange Arabic on the window.

It is seated at a table full of Ruths
in the senior living community.

The sacred, I tell her,
is the reason she shouldn't
beat herself up so much about
beating herself up so much.

Holy how a child's tears itch
a tiny bit as they dry on my cheek.

God is what I tell time.

The Music Garden, If I Built It

First,
broad swath of field,
rye grass? wheat?
leading to ocean or large large lake,
lake with horizon as shore.

The vista
approached
through a sweet curving tunnel,
poplar trees, or elms
touching tips overhead.

Add invocations
of old-fashioned things:

charm of the names of the crushes
of grade school,
a list each visitor
adds to
in chalk.

At the center
of a spiral,
a statue of Diarmid,
the Irish warrior
blessed by the fairy
so women who looked at him
loved him, fast, deeply:
theme and variations
on her curse,
his afflictions.

Here, build a salmon stream,
spawning time, rocketing,
the urge, universal,
for homecoming, rutting,
birth, death, the usual.

Hummingbird feeders hang
in full sun, to conjure that hope
for nerve-wracking gemstones.

In the shade now, slower
now, a table, two chairs,
two glasses of wine,
to make life look glossy.

An empty dirt circle,
thick walls of bamboo
played by the wind.
Green thicket clacking,
heart attack smacking,
black stone in the middle
to spin on. Begin.

At the exit, plant buddleia,
lantana and phlox,
for calling all butterflies,
each wingflick and nectaring
a brand new idea,

dandle out to the street,
and repeat.
And repeat.

2

PENNY ON THE SIDEWALK

"Expose for the Flame"

advice given to a New York Times *photographer*
when shooting a space shuttle takeoff

We believe nothing
is more valuable
than disaster.

We have learned
good news
is not news.

This shrinks
my own sweet
aperture.

Will I see
what does not
flame out?

Will I love
what isn't
first-ever?

Will I tire
of the daily,
regular real?

Will I fight
that raw need for new
whenever I come home?

With who knows what.
When where
knows why.

Toward Teaching a One-Year-Old to Pray

A shiny-dime day,
I learn how kites fit in the wind.
At the height of birdflight
God shines brighter than otters,
than knuckles of sculptures
everyone pats for good luck.

I can see human existence, splotchy
and beaten down like the sole under
the insole, accumulating without end,
soft greasy dust on the grill around
the fan. Humans, before they shed
their skin, look goofy and inaccurate
like the photos of them dancing.

What if bodies, buried, descended
to the center, wind chimes in the solid
air of an empty living room? Here,
the good news is written, how big?
so big! in mother-of-pearl ink,
and we share a new pulse. Visit
the woman who left flowers daily
on a different empty subway car.

Kate's eyes widen even in the shore gusts.
Time, a peaceful curtain, rolls over
a planet as neat as a funeral home.
Alation, the state of having wings, elation,
so close. Love her, she delights at the kite
before ever understanding string or wind.

The Pornography of Recent Times

What did the rainwater taste like
in the middle of the Atlantic
on an explorer's ship centuries ago?

In a paneled room
the insides of trees
face you down—

the equivalent, a wallcovering of our sagittal sections.

What you require to thrive—
soap needs water, we need everything and time—
wears you down.

If only this world became a black-chinned hummingbird's nest,
a flaxen cup that expands and flattens
as the young ones grow.

Purple martins are dying.

As the summer ages
a breast usually plump looks bony.
If only we hadn't sprayed, the bird wouldn't shake so.

Stares you down—
tigers feel happy when well-fed and won't mate unless happy.
This one was born here

(he'll mount his mother so they put her on The Pill)

pacing up and down
the right angles of cages
in a square damp city.

Fugue after Writing Headlines

When I think of the chemicals we put
in the breastmilk of dolphins, when I
walk in acid rain, swim in acid sea, visit
the edges of mineshafts in the state park

where Ford dumped lakes of car paint,
when I smell leachate of landfill, tailings
from mountaintops, see indelible taint,
scarred hand of abused infant, loyal lover

left alone, garden untended, grave sunken,
what if an asteroid t-boned us at nine a.m.?
No time to be startled. Suddenly shriven.
A get-out-of-hell-free card. A karmic kiss.

Come, holy hunk of mineral.
Give us rest, a silent funeral.

Tuesday Afternoon Metaphysics Lesson

Today Kate said she was drawing an angry ghost.
I asked what's he mad at?
"Me," she said.
Why?
"Cause I'm drawing him."

How Heisenberg-y, as if
a spirit had hovered in the molecules
of her blue crayon tip who could've emerged
in any old emotional state, if that dimpled
fist had not borne down so hard.

And I know if I ask why she's drawing him
she will holler, "yer buggin' me!" so I just answer
what comes after G, why H, and how to draw the S.
And we place the labeled picture on the fridge,
that altar to preschool power, to delineation itself.

Bob and Sally Laminate Are Moving Out

You've seen them. They arrive in your brand new picture frames.
They live in This High Retreat surrounded by tall arrangements
of flowers that bloom in different climates. The vases and faucets shine
as if lit from above. Bob and Sally, piano-teacher prim, have no trouble
keeping this apartment forever company-ready. No need to call ahead.
Sal stands above the necessities of soap dish and scrub brush. Her tea towels
have hospital corners. His toothbrush and toothpaste live in another borough.
The hangers each take two inches, evenly spaced, on the racks in the closets.

They are not us. But we will pretend to live like them for a few days,
at least until we have to find the stamps, the 401(k) signup sheets, the baby.
We play at looking as spiffy as our own done dry cleaning (where did *that* go?)
and smelling like the cider and cinnamon sticks we simmer during open houses.
The windows are always up and Aspen clean, every light on. We scrubbed
each scuff, painted every ding, wished we'd done it years ago. But we miss
messiness—to splay, mark turf, jump to the next project before cleaning up.
There is delight in that. Besides, our hearts moved to the new place weeks ago.

Advance Directive

You know when you carry a load of wash
without a basket and drop eight things,

one by one, getting to the bedroom? That
is how it starts. Without blood, my mood.

Fluorescent lights buzz, the walls all beige.
I'd wanted to go turquoise instead of gray.

I'd wanted to spend these years watching
the fountain with a soundtrack, the one

that rockets twelve stories high, crowded
with children. Or I could've been happy

tracking honeybees all summer long,
listening to Vaughan Williams, spending

Easter in a different country every year.
No such luck. The generator next door

sounds like a hovering copter. All day.
I used to know the magic trick. Now I look

for one card in the deck. I'm erased.
Goldfish see everything anew, a merciful

protection from boredom. Make me a fish.
Talking for me, you dare to know what I

can't say. Let that old cat run off. Sell
all the dishes. When I've gone to solitude,

plant a blueberry bush over me. Bake a pie.
Put me in your password for remembrance.

The Last Christmas My Daughter Won't Know about Sex

She says she doesn't want a boyfriend "because you have to pay him too much."
(She didn't hear that from me.) From the basement I hear her upstairs,
pursuing the perfect round-off, pound the floor, stick it, Ta-da! Chin high,
flattest chest extended, arms embracing applause from Olympic viewers

yet unborn. She doesn't know that once you sleep with him, you fall for him
harder, even if you shouldn't. She doesn't know she will feel miserable
for at least a year after each person she loves so much dies. Santa's still invited
with cookies and notes, but eyed suspiciously by friends with older brothers.

She asks about my dad, "If you're dead, can you think? Can you dream?"
She hasn't wondered why tomorrow and sorrow rhyme. She doesn't get
why we giggled at the billboard in Delaware, "Hooters—Tuesdays!

Kids Eat Free!" She says, "You basically feel like you're reading a book
in your dream" and "If I didn't have a crazy mom I would die." I think,
damn, she could tame alligators, but not boys, with those eyes.

The Asshole's Cat

I'm washing behind my ears, inside the only chain-link fence
in the cul-de-sac, eyes closing slowly as he plays his music just
that loud. Even I know the songs sound old and angry. I heard the cop.
I know why he shuts it off at 9:59 weeknights, 11:59 on weekends.

Yes, he will report you for trespassing if you knock on his door
to ask him to turn it down. Yes, he's the one who trashed the tulips,
snapped them, not cut them, left them to wilt. That's what you get.
And yes, back in more cordial days, he borrowed gas mowers

and returned them empty. I don't mind the late action movies
played to rattle the windows, or the way he sits out tanning flab
just to force you to look at him. I get that. I caterwaul in my way, too.
I once sat on his belly while he tried to watch TV in bed. Once.

The other cats don't stop by anymore, but I'm at peace.
He feeds me, and when I ran off for a week, he cried.

Still Life with Ice Sculpture and Candles

dedicated to babs,
with babs knows what
and babs knows why

—DON MARQUIS

I have chosen my Omega Male, the last, the one
I won't need another one after. I'd tried the Alphas, eh.

So we do not eat the candy heart without reading it.
The fortune cookie we shared announced
"You have an enviable marriage."

That's true, after dad's death, ma's move, head lice,
your family's fits, our hour-long commutes,
daughter who says no, son who says maybe not,
the fighting between them I couldn't survive
if you didn't supply slapstick solutions.

You opened the fungal cream box,
read aloud the possible adverse reactions:
shortness of breath, fever, joint pain, fainting,
swelling of face, hives, weight gain, severe headache,
menstrual irregularities, fast pulse, nausea, intestinal ulcers,
vertigo, difficulty falling asleep, abnormal hair growth, glaucoma,
vomiting,
death.

It sounds, my love, like growing old,
what we vowed to do together. Doable, no?

We'll have to pardon the future now. It will challenge us.
But we have survived the first yawn during a kiss.
We've chosen the word *perennate* as our own: to live over
from one harvest season to another. In between crises
and naps and new pets, turbulence is mostly unexpected,
the stewardess said. So we grow, roots and canopy,
higher, deeper, aiming for always,
a wave tossing foam in the sun.

Rain. Saturday Morning. Training Wheels.

We're far from the seventeen flavors of hell
I run across in the course of my week,
things that are just never good: glue traps,

outgrown swing sets, waiting rooms, a cut
chapter, ignored subpoenas, the endodontist,
hospital cafeteria, durable power of attorney.

And yes, it's raining but it's not ninety degrees
like it's been for weeks, so the drops form
a lukewarm shower, the most refreshing kind.

I'm teaching her you're not a true outdoorswoman
unless you go out in bad weather. She teaches me
puddle time: downpours are inherently funny.

Penny on the sidewalk. Barely needed training wheels.
Getting stuck half-way through giant puddles.
The rooster tail of the water when she pedals so hard.

She's teaching me joy, but I'm teaching her joy,
and the dog, who hasn't a lick of retriever in him,
shakes and looks at us as if we need to go in. We don't.

3

GHOSTS OF GOOD NEWS

Building a Better Bivalve

. . . a group of investors has licensed technology developed by Rutgers to produce a sexless oyster that grows faster and meatier than oysters in the wild.

—THE NEW YORK TIMES, JUNE 12, 2005

Hello, paradise seed!
To your health, passion-tossed!
To eat you is one holy immersion.

But no. Passion's tossed out of the shell.

I live in a remodeled obstetrician's office,
haunted in happy ways,
ghosts of good news received.

On our honeymoon we paddled
through a school of chum salmon
suiciding upstream, grating
sides raw between

streambed and sun,
dying to procreate. They looked like
fifteen-year-old cars with sixteen-year-old drivers,
parking, pressuring, rocking.

Astronauts do it. Mermaids do, too.
Female dragonflies put up with males
who pierce skull holes for foreplay.
Male bees die with eviscerated afterglow.

So I'd like my oysters skinnier and hornier, please,
coming together, pearl-moist,
bay-tasting, cove-tasting,
dancing the fruitfulness tango.

Liking Drew

When I conceived the second time, I had sure ideas about him,
that he was *seeing* through me, that the landscape I took in on that hike
by the pass—cliff, lake, underside of hill—became crucial to his nurturance.

I felt he was a boy, or a girl who would resemble her father.
I listened to crickets slowing down, like a music box or old dog,
and prepared for the winter work of growing the new heartbeat.

I watched the reflections from my sunlit engagement ring
on the newspaper, like the spinning universe on a ballroom floor,
and how I could unite them, tilting them in to one central spark.

He is greater than the sum of all previous birthday wishes,
the big little boy, seeming older, more complete, more knowing.
His tongue trembles when he smiles, as if he's laughing first

at jokes we'll share three years from now. Maybe he'll help teach me
about my unknown ancestors—that it's in this blood to love the wide open,
the downs, Palouse, Long Meadow. That their people watch hard,

locking onto the eagle flying across the lake, past the moment it disappears.
That smiles bubble up, insistently, from no known source. He becomes
the family's Reclining Buddha, all fat and happy on his side, asleep, serene.

New parents break plates, glasses, stemware. Because they get tired,
yes, but because they fear breaking the baby, dropping, damning
him to eternal slowness. They chip china instead.

Hold tight. His sister asked a tough one the other day, harder than
Is the lightning right side up, Mama? She wanted to know *Why is one first?*
And we wondered if she resented her birth order. Surely mad at her parents.

Mama walked with her baby on the beach later and noticed it took only two waves
to erase my footprints, two generations, children, grandchildren, to forget me
and my humor. I knew nothing really of Nanny, my great-grandmother.

And now how I wanted grandchildren, too. More to look out of, from inside.

Done Procreating

With this new beginning I sense a certain end.
No more happy visits to the hospital, ever.
Loss takes over the tell-all-friends news: the folks selling
the family homestead, the dog, the cat put down after outlasting
seven romances, the inevitable deaths now that we expect
no more birthing. And who would fall for me now,
cut off from all old flames who showed signs of peskiness,
bruisy rings under my eyes from the five a.m. feeding, impy haircut
requiring no grooming time, since I have none? Last maternity
leave, no plans to move to a new house, no chance of travel. But

I love his blueberry eyes, such a dark gray, and when I looked
in them last night I could see how I look to him—my pale skin,
my face, and behind it, the headboard. In Drew's little world,
where every square foot, every three-hour wakening, startles,
a smile travels high into his scalp, fills the room deep like a ghost.

Spoon Song

The notes sound sad and whole, a cream of tone.
The foghorn stops but the sun does not come out.
Everything's always next, and nothing's now.
"Did his heart fall asleep?" Kate asks about Grampa.

Who knew I'd feel so sad to feed you, baby boy,

to watch carrots drip from rubbery spoon and mouth,
stain the bunny shirt? And to go back to work
with this sweetness barely tasted? Wave bye-bye.
Later on from someone else you'll learn forks and clapping.

I feel the worldwide weight of dust settling on the sea.

We discover our loved ones over again, backwards.
The slipknot Dad tied on balloons, absent, ruined July 4th.
The buckeyes he'd hand me every walk, emptied the fall.
He won't know this child as much as I'd like. Neither will I.

Drew's Abject Love of Dinosaurs

Do mosquitoes pick their noses?
If all the people died would the dinosaurs come back?
And are Conehead and Strongneck and Longneck friends?

He sounds so very certain that his triceratops, heavy, impossible
to pack, with triple-spiked tail, tree-trunk legs, pure XY
chromosomes, trumps my small-hands tyrannosaurus every time.

I do want to share my boy's love of Jurassic hard-plastic monsters.
After watching one of his movies, I think of a dinosaur
falling in love one warm spring day under the conifers of Pangaea,

the leathery smell of crushed horsetails rising green from the ground.
I feel in my small intestine that ounce of tenderness certainly
there, then, cloaca to cloaca, a soft lurch at winter's end, to reproduce.

In his favorite museum gallery, I learn they moved
in herds, even. But they snarl and fight, eat raw meat,
these cold-blooded hockey players, gory, foreign to me,

while my blond buddy with the baseball-card smile
runs all male, legs wide, elbows bent, fast, then looks
three stories up, to terrible lizard skull, announcing:

"Mama, the *T. rex* is smiling."

Solo Prelude, on "Love Divine"

pink rose on the altar
a peaceable family
Episcopal childhood
a dying grandmother
the smell of old spice wood
a decade of Sunday School
weeknights spent reading.

a summer in England
the soaring of downs
the truth of last century
shadows slide downhill
a peck of fresh strawberries
old port, its helium
the books and the learning.

the starched shirt, the bridegroom
the kneeling together
twice hope for the future
the laughing and spinning,
serving, adopting,
coaching, encouraging,
embracing, long whispering.

baptism, another one,
the rote, daunting liturgy
tantrums before Sunday School
but getting to Sunday School
one ounce of pure beauty
one ounce of divinity
come down in this music.

That First Week after the Last Day of School

The day has the pace of the tangle pulled out of a brush,
wafting to the grass. The backyard's the everything room,
the always room. We mix clover and privet to make June.
Cardinal's a hole in the blue-green world, a hole red tears through.

They ask, "What if the moon turned inside out?"
Thanks for the reminder to think this way.

I am transcribing the wind chime music with them, one color per note.
Cloud shadows piebald the hill. The cardinal sounds like a tambourine.
We discuss the geometric patterns on our eyelids as we sunbathe.
Down with Ceaser! she writes in her play. Things that end are mean.

We'll drink from the sprinkler, we decide.
It's too hot out now, too far to go inside.

Someone Scratched *Hope* on the Trail

The name and an arrow pointed back to where we started.
Are winter trees pretty like bald women, stark, revealing
unsuspected views? I like woods in the winter, but he thinks
everything looks dead. I won't agree, won't find the world

ugly four months of the year, won't imagine the rows of men
tied and blindfolded and shot, dumped by thugs in the river.
I hear March is when the bodies of suicides float home.

Why these lightbulb-hot thoughts? Hope went behind us.
Our children are sliding away, small planes seen from a jet

lumbering above. Soon they'll talk to us just minutes a week.

But what if we'd approached that piece of path from the north,

toasted each other with buoyancy instead? We would have
time, and a place for everything, everything in its place,

camping gear in the back seat, paying for gas not home repairs,
an itinerary of national parks and trophy trout streams, pensions
paying us to hike and find poetry and bass in ponds and paths,

reading the same books, discussing them, rutting in daylight,
relearning to cook, staying with friends, only as long as we want,
living near the kids, babysitting to give tired parents weekends off,
fully enjoying each other, in sunshine, without locks, seeing, at last,

Hope is a woman whose friends leave directions.

I Heard She Had a Recurring Nightmare of Fetal Skeletons Standing Upright

I had a vision of a car smashing into a Sunday paper,
shooting shreds of the week everywhere. Rain-soaked scraps
would still show up years later, reminders of what happened
at the Bensons' backyard during the party, when everyone
was eating talking laughing and no one was watching Anna.
She wandered off and fell in the pond and drowned

and they filled in the pond and what would grow there?
Nothing. Ever. But mists gathered. And deer stood
and stared at the house the Bensons could never leave.
We planted bamboo to hide the view, but that didn't help.
In paintings of crucifixions, so often the hands lie flat, palms
forward, at rest, falsely peaceful. Gnarled fingers, clenched

with veins and tendons popping, that's more true.
No flat field hiding benthic loss, endless grief.

I Am Pamela Pan

He ran away the day he was born, after
hearing us discussing what a fine man
he would be. We never saw him again.
I do not know his face. I've lost my shadow.

I learn about him from the mockingbirds,
how he lived with fairies in Kensington Gardens.
But he is not a lost boy, he knows where he is.
He chose a different way, the *second* to the right.

The birds say red hair, green rags, flight like a finch's.
They cannot tell me if he has my husband's chin,
as I suspect, or his able hands. My boy can never know
I am the green in his eyes, and I tell fine stories.

He's the towel I cry into when the hanky's too small.
He is my straight on till morning, every night.
He will never grow up or get bored. He will never marry.
Instead, he is "youth and joy," he tells Hook, "a little bird

that has broken out of the egg." I'm the shattered shell,
in irretrievable pieces, a droughtland of shards.
I had more children, daughters, thankfully—
they tend to stay around. I am afraid to tell them

I lost their brother, they'll think me careless.
But one can't hold back a magic wish, especially
when it wants to share itself. One can't grasp glee
and mischief. It's easier to grab hold of a minute ago.

Here in Alwaysland the taxes and maids must be paid,
the dinners earned and cleaned up, the corners tucked.
The stories repeat themselves, the births, the funerals.
Perhaps he was right to go. I miss him so.

4.

ILLEGIBLE SMILES

Wheeled Walker on the Bottom of the Ocean

Dandled by currents, slow long descent
like sun syruping down a web strand,
slipping to moon's dark side, it lands
on four feet, ten thousand feet down.

The bottom, ruined like the train's quiet car
by an eternal piece of junk. Anything lurks
in shadows to steal the widow's wedding ring.
Sand specks float in robot glare.

My mother can't talk, but I call her every night,
tell her about my day, pretend she is who she was,
because she may be, and why guess wrong?

The sea floor moves in "mass wasting
events"—landslides, flows, falls. We dump
a whale carcass, gauge erosion, see plastic bags
slithering round. Buckets, monofilament, a tire
that spun on desert roads, now cold, dark, still.
Unexploded bombs, a bed pan, mop head.
The helmet of someone killed in it.

After she dies, I may keep calling, talk to the dark.

We make up words for the unfathomable. There is one—
infaunal—for deep sea creatures of the soft sea bottom.
Palilalia, the repetition of one's own spoken words.
A word for measuring water depth: *bathymetry*.
Depth of dark, pressure, love. Night.

The dropped crab pot and tangled net keep killing,
mindless as cancer, no lines to the surface, no use.

The Squandered

The window boxes unwatered, eighty dollars of daisies
dry and dead like the smoky afterimages of fireworks,

the fireworks over too soon because I wished and wished
for the finale, the hikes postponed until Nextember.

The cross I lost on the playground, gold, great-grandmother's,
a present for First Holy Communion, the Raggedy Ann, dropped.

Neglected toys with battery acid crystallizing around the edges,
the hours of babies I should've watched instead of newscasts,

the mealy peach, still gorgeous, left too long, the midnights
I could have slept but my mind had a sheen on it, ears ringing.

That feeling of having forgotten every insight from every class,
every plot of every novel, title of movie, figure from history.

Am I glad the week has passed, am I wishing my minutes
away, those planets that barely glow, that no one sees?

The Kids Play at the Shelter, Two Friday Nights after Little G Shot Himself under the Boardwalk

Simon says play.
The kids say how.
No one ever said.

Simon says do the robot.
Simon says do the robot while whistling Happy Birthday.
The robot dancers giggle.
OK stop.
Simon didn't say stop.

Simon says keep up with your plan. Tanika laughs.
Little G had said he got expended from school but
Lamarr said last month Little G finally wasn't cursing the birds for chirping.

Gary said you ain't never gonna amount to nothing.
Gary said come here girl and turn out that light.
Gary said do what I say.
Gary said put your hands on my hips.
Gary said shut up. And then mmmmmm.
Gary said if you tell I'm gonna do that to Rafa too.
Gary never said Simon says.
Tanika never said nothing.

Simon says get your photo ID.
Simon says take off your doo-rag.
Simon says get your birth certificate and social.

Little G came back to Lamarr, sat on his bed
glowing all weird, and says do what I did.
Little G says I'm in your head now.
Little G says it doesn't hurt.
Lamarr says shut up, Little G.
Little G says it's easier this way.
Little G says but you'll never know coz you're too chicken.
Little G says you know you feel as tired as I did.
Little G says quit faking that smile, it's not all right.
Lamarr says, loud, don't play with me yo.
Simon didn't hear.

Lamarr says when I wake up I feel like I have no purpose.
Lamarr says when I was five I saw my mother kill herself.
Lamarr says I had thirty-four foster placements.
Lamarr says I'm gay and celibate. Celibate, as if it's not hard enough
being black and Cherokee and a mutt and orphaned and beaten up
and Southern and gay.
Celibate. Jesus.

Lamarr says you should give that baby girl up for adoption, Tanika.
Tanika says give your own damn self up for adoption, Lamarr.
Simon says you're too old.

Simon says did you go to your meeting?
Simon says do you need an interview suit?
Simon says you're going to be great.
Simon didn't say. Simon did.

Little G said I'm going to the Underwood Hotel.
Lamarr said that's just the sand under the boardwalk, yo.
Little G said I don't care, it's home.
Simon says come back as soon as you can.
Little G said yeah whatevs.

Lamarr says Little G's dad said you cost too much to feed, sound familiar?
Lamarr says I am never going to do shit like that to a child and excuse my language.

Simon didn't say it would be easy.
Simon says believe in yourself.
Simon says I do.

Little G said I'm out of here.
Simon couldn't say.

The Dark Side of Selene, the Moon

White things go away last,
teeth in an animal flattened on the road,
the chalked line where the body fell,
me.

And my light, white and numb
like the eyes of dead fish.

Most nights I come down through the dark sky of earth
and I kiss him slowly, reluctantly, fitfully,
the way someone's head moves
as she falls asleep on a bus.

I caress him reverently, gently,
with the peaceful pace of paddleboats,
seeming to preclude all evil,
no wars ever fought in them, hush.

I can caress him, but to go further would shame me,
so I feel constantly, feverishly ready. Can't even
nap next to him, so we'd have something in common,
and I can't leave him for someone else, not after what I did.

Confession: I put Endymion to sleep. He wasn't even suffering,
was just a peaceful shepherd boy, but too gorgeous to live.
I lulled him, the slow relaxation of hair being rinsed, his space
ever intimate, safe and silver as a snow-covered car.

Sometimes I console myself that I've given him
the hugest gift, immortality. But he's dead, for all he knows.
Where did you get your "blest is his fortune," Theocritus?
My shrink wants to know if my father seemed domineering,

if I had any family history of necrophilia or narcolepsy.
She'd turn me in to the authorities,
but she knows better than to cross me.
I can't print what my girlfriends say, vicious stuff,

though they envy me for having someone who doesn't insist
on being early to every train, who doesn't point out
how the restaurant I chose didn't get good reviews at all.
But as a lover, mine's about as dynamic as a cast-iron

lawn deer. Of course, I take full responsibility for this.
I've tried the wake-him-with-a-kiss trick, but it failed.
If you saw him, maybe you'd understand why I did it,
a face as clear and placid as water in a bowl.

Museum quality. As handsome as everyone's
first love and favorite snapshot of themselves
combined. But all that's left inside is the vacuum
of the light of a star gone out, emptiness,

every instant chasing what used to be,
always farther away, so much farther so fast.

In Appreciation for the Uniformity of Physical Bodies

After nine days of dividing, each human embryo develops a right and a left side,
just after separating into placenta and amniotic sac, long before the heart beats.
The axis the primary fact, and next the uniformity of us all, everywhere,
our four limbs, our central head, our upper and our lower, our finite senses.

But it's not always this way, believe me. I have just returned from a world
where bodies vary, person to person, lover to lover. They saw my symmetry
as deformity, a physical lack of imagination, while they gleefully sprayed
their graffiti to all heights, depending on where their appendages sprouted.

Their road signs hung at many levels, for various eyes. Some had binocular
vision, some had hearts as fast as voles', and some embraced neoteny, adults
keeping childlike characteristics; others looked middle-aged from puberty.
Noses, if present, had the varied, personal shapes of well-used lipsticks.

Some had so many parts, some washable, some dry clean only, that they kept fresh
only through wind baths. Each had his own musical instrument, built for the distance
between mouth-like area and finger-like area, however far apart those would sprout.

Thus no symphonies came down through the canon, just an endless art of improv.
Some, like our blue whale, owned hearts bigger than Volkswagens. They differed
day to day, like the retelling of a dream. A few developed the elegant power

of big-footed kicking, swimming without flippers, seldom needing breath.
All genitals stayed private: some hid themselves in the down-the-drain way
a snake's tail disappears, some looked like police sketches, bits described
separately. As the creatures paired off—when some got married they joined

into one body—no one could predict the flow of the couplings, or where a baby would emerge. The midwives were the wisest, most respected among them. At the end of life, each individual burst, not passed, away.

But I have come home, gladly. I am back, to hold and touch and love and praise the right and the left of you, your center, your strong back and muscled calves that compare so favorably to other men's, the fact of your core and handedness and your balance, and the way we fit together, in snugness, in tune, in time.

The Inarticulate Man Who Tries

—to Jimmy Stewart

When you sat in our parlor, originally Nana's,
fire in the fireplace, grandfather clock tocking
contralto, sharing your dreams for all things
clean, involving the underdog's triumph, I saw

something slack and sensuous around the mouth,
plus that nose straighter than mine, and wanted.
You mentioned how the censors forbade you
to sing "you'd be . . . so sweet to waken with,

so nice to sit down to eggs and bacon with."
You don't act, you react, you said. I'm that
small-town girl born to dance. Why didn't I
give you anything to respond to, just touch

that navy blue and gold tie, just to smooth it,
once? I should have asked, what happens
when your stunt pilot dies, what did the letter
say, that your father gave you before the war,

the one you carried those three years? Mother came
downstairs; you had to be going. After the thin man
left, the man who knew too much, the rare breed,
I poked at the fire, a woman who'd said too little.

For the Life of Me

Jammed solar panels,
an outfling of spring action,
a torn umbilical, and now.

In my gloves, fingertip heaters
I control one by one. My EKG
reaches surgeons in Houston.

I have two cubic feet of air.
I have seven and a half hours.

Look at that planet, swaddled in
the worldwide quiet of about-to-snow.
Does the Atlantic taste like the Pacific?
I never knew.

But I know you are watching, love,
wondering about letting the kids watch, too.
Don't.

The scrambled rescue attempt,
the anchorman's intoning,
won't make it easier.

How do flags ever fly full-staff?
Each year we use enough coffin steel
to build a Golden Gate Bridge.

Maybe I'm a frozen and forgotten
embryo or a voicemail, on the phone
of a missing person. Millions

picture themselves here, the nowhere
vacuum, 275 degrees. No dolphin
to dandle me up. I'll wash up on no shore.

I wave, all I can do,
more hello than goodbye now,
thirty minutes in. I howl at the earth.

Really, aren't you all like me,
missing your bed, your dog,
dying in front of everyone?

We had such a great time dressing up, having Fun, and Dancing to 50s music!

…but the traumatic underpinnings of life are not specific to any generation. The first day of school and the first day in an assisted-living facility are remarkably similar.

—"The Trauma of Being Alive," *The New York Times*, August 3, 2013

Everyone else went to orientation.
Am I getting too old for my favorite things?
My pretty pink dishes, twelve of them. Where is Buddy?

All the hallways look the same, tan.
Someone put the shovels and buckets away.
Let's have another tea party, the wet sounds of lips,

warm chatter. But everyone else
can move faster and remember instructions.
I used to manage fine, home, used to tie my shoes fast enough.

Here they know different card games.
They can all make it to the bathroom, every time.
Unpryable milk cartons. Illegible smiles. I miss Mother.

I Talk to My Twin, 38 Weeks Gestation

Birth's the end of it all, you're sure.
No one has come back, you say.
You mock me for believing in life
after delivery, in mother, in love.

You have never seen or smelled her.
But I know her by heart, her heart,
bass drum surrounding our snares.
She's all around us, warm, sloshing.

You ponder the empty next.
The cord is too short, you say.
We won't be able to move.
Tiny hopes just rise and die,

and I'm a fool to think there's
anything beyond what we know.
But I know we will outgrow this
tight scrum. Light will be more

than on/off, every inch we grow
is a step closer to new splendor.
We will hear her songs unmuffled.
Life after birth will engulf, delight.

And after that, a third dimension
for the color wheel. Foreign music.
Do not rest in peace, beloved. Soar,
gambol, joke, be busy, string jewel

words, exalt, exult. Who is sure death
isn't a brighter world to emerge into?

  —in honor of Elise Partridge 1958–2015

National Oblivion Awareness Day

I still can't find the letters Dad wrote
for me to read after he died, a pile he'd add to
occasionally and tell me about, and I wouldn't
want to hear, so I didn't listen. No, I did, he put them
in the safe deposit box, then in a red folder on the desk.
Now, nowhere.

Is it all a string of missed joy—the meteor shower clouded over,
the unopened chocolate molds I forgot to use with my kids?
I never made that plaster cast of me holding the baby's hand.
Is his sister too old for me to give her the doll I'd felt too old for?

What if our desks held pictures
of what our loved ones look like
ten years from now?

The first parent to die gets to smile from more frames,
his memory polished by grief and adoration, more people
around to dread Christmas because he died just before it.

Maybe I know what Dad must've written. He rests
in peace in the part of me that can still sleep.

Love Poem to the Seattle Compline Choir

Light fades through the plain windows
of this concrete cathedral as twelve men file in
slowly, music held across monk-like bellies.
The young people bring pillows and blankets,

overflow onto the floor. (What parent says
no when asked permission to go to *church*?)
Which man sings prettiest, which one highest?
What day jobs do angel-men-singers hold?

Do they teach, or heal, do they tally numbers?
Do they gather at parties for a cappella choirs,
are they celebrities, favored by women?
Now deep-blue panes, some grayer than others,

fade in stately rhythm through the darkening
spectrum, royal, navy, pewter, battleship,
storm sky, midnight, through opaque glass
as we ask for a quiet night, a peaceful end.

Remember the thin one with the long ponytail
who looked like he studied philosophy? Would
he gather me into his arms if I explained
how he and his equals conjured each week

a giant spinning column of pure beauty,
bringing tears of awe, reminiscences stuck
among the stanzas: ethics, ancestors, gospels,
a half-hour vortex of holiness in this concrete

box-like house of hope? I return each year
from across the continent, blessed each time
by their building descant closing the day.
Outside, I smell not just the sea, but the salmon.

FINALE

Charmed

Let all things, seen and unseen
Their notes of gladness blend

—HYMN LYRICS, JOHN OF DAMASCUS, 750 A.D.

Why does anyone have to leave a world so stunning?
A world serving up breakfast all day, diamonds
forged from cremains, cirrus clouds to overlook
from a plane, frost fairs on the frozen River Thames,

world with haiku hiding in the clouds, specific angels
overseeing only honey, only tenth birthdays, where,
standing in the right fountain, you can see a rainbow
ring bloom from your feet, world with truffle salt,

with the bright lines that river water flings on tree trunks,
a world that lets you drive the clotted roads of the carpool,
and gives you the relief of turning really loud music down,
where if you're sick, people you know turn cussedly kind,

making it harder than ever to leave, a world where you may,
with any luck, die on a screen porch on a warm, windy day?

NOTES

Letter Written with the Kruger Brothers Picking in the Background: with a huge debt to their song "Up 18 North."

Love Song to Boredom: The Pascal quote is from *Pensées*. "...like a snapshot of one instant, forever," is from Professor José Senovilla of the University of the Basque Country in Bilbao, Spain, quoted in *The New Scientist*, December 18, 2007. The photographer is Josh Haner, in a *New York Times* blog, "On the Campaign Trail in Iowa."

Building a Better Bivalve: Thank you, weird spammers, for the first two lines.

The Inarticulate Man Who Tries: With gratitude for Diane Lockward's poetry prompt, and IMDb.com, for Mr. Stewart's filmography.

We had such a great time dressing up, having Fun, and Dancing to 50s music!: The title comes from Bickford Senior Living's blog about resident activities.

I Talk to My Twin, 38 Weeks Gestation: Based on a legend that ran rampant on the internet, attributed both to Hungarian writer Útmutató a Léleknek and to Czech psychologist Jirina Prekop, Ph.D.

Lines from Cole Porter's "Easy to Love" are used with permission from the Cole Porter estate.

"On Leaving the Newsroom" is used with permission from *The New York Times*.

With gratitude to my parents, to readers Tom, Lynn, Rams, Marty, Jude, the Montclair workshop, the Gonk, Liss, Frith, Trisha, Elise, and Sarah, and to editors who say yes.

ACKNOWLEDGMENTS

Alaska Quarterly Review: "Wheeled Walker on the Bottom of the Ocean"

Belletrist: "The Asshole's Cat," "The Kids Play at the Shelter, Two Friday Nights after Little G Shot Himself under the Boardwalk," "Rain. Saturday Morning. Training Wheels."

Beloit Poetry Journal: "The Pornography of Recent Times"

Broken Lines—The Art & Craft of Poetry: "The Possible Utility of Poets"

Connecticut Review: "Expose for the Flame"

Crab Creek Review: "For the Life of Me," "In Appreciation for the Uniformity of Physical Bodies," "Spoon Song," "Yawp"

The Crafty Poet: "The Inarticulate Man Who Tries," "My Man, the Green Man"

Cream City Review: "The Dark Side of Selene, the Moon"

Ekleksographia: "The Last Christmas My Daughter Won't Know about Sex"

The Final Lilt of Songs: "Building a Better Bivalve"

Fine Madness: "Bob and Sally Laminate Are Moving Out"

Fire on Her Tongue: "Done Procreating"

Intimacy: "I Talk to My Twin, 38 Weeks Gestation"

Journal of New Jersey Poets: "Abloom & Awry," "Drew's Abject Love of Dinosaurs," "I Heard She Had a Recurring Nightmare of Fetal Skeletons Standing Upright," "Letter Written with the Kruger Brothers Picking in the Background," "Liking Drew," "Love Song to Boredom," "The Meadow Saffron Said My Best Days Fled," "National Oblivion Awareness Day," "The Next Creation of the Universe," "Solo Prelude, on 'Love Divine,'" "Someone Scratched *Hope* on the Trail"

NYTimes.com: "On Leaving the Newsroom"

One: "Music Is an Underground River That Needs to Be Discovered"

Poetry East: "Charmed," "Covalent," "That First Week after the Last Day of School," "Theophany, or Staying Home from Church to Write," "Toward Teaching a One-Year-Old to Pray," "The Squandered"

Southwest Review: "I am Pamela Pan"

Stillwater Review: "Fugue after Writing Headlines"

US 1 Worksheets: "Still Life with Ice Sculptures and Candles," "Tuesday Afternoon Metaphysics Lesson"

The poem "Abloom & Awry" won the 2014 New Jersey Poets Prize.

CAVANKERRY'S MISSION

CavanKerry Press is committed to expanding the reach of poetry to a general readership by publishing poets whose works explore the emotional and psychological landscapes of everyday life.

Text for this book has been set in Chaparral Pro—an old-style font with slab serif influences—which was created by Adobe type designer Carol Twombly in 1997.